THE CHARITABLE REMAINDER TRUST

Reduce Estate and Income Taxes Through Charitable Giving

By
Adam Starchild

Books for Business
New York - Hong Kong

The Charitable Remainder Trust:
Reduce Estate and Income Taxes Through
Charitable Giving

by
Adam Starchild

ISBN: 0-89499-243-0

Books for Business
New York - Hong Kong
http://www.BusinessBooksInternational.com

Contents

Contents

The Charitable Remainder Trust — Too Good to Be True?

What Is a "CRT"?

This chapter will acquaint you with the near magical possibilities of a tax-saving, income-producing legal device known as a "charitable remainder trust" or "CRT." Although "CRT" is the currently popular term, these trusts are also known as "life income" and "wealth accumulation" trusts. Both descriptions are accurate — and therein lies the money magic.

A CRT is just the thing for a person who wants to avoid capital gains taxes on appreciated property, in pursuit of increased retirement income or seeking estate tax relief. But this trust is also the perfect vehicle to achieve your personal philanthropic goals, while also helping yourself and your family. In fact, while tax savings and income enhancement are central attractions of the CRT, the chief motivation should be the settlor/donor's charitable intentions. After all, when the final distribution of trust assets is made — and they can have considerable value — the charity of your choice will be the major beneficiary.

In the meantime, there is no reason why the objects of your generosity cannot reward their benefactor with a seat on your

1

church board of trustees, or your alma mater's establishment of a scholarship bearing your name.

What It Can Do for You

Here is what the creation of a CRT can accomplish for you. Properly drafted, formulated and managed, a charitable remainder trust is an excellent "transfer tax" avoidance instrumentality that can —

- avoid completely any capital gains tax payment on your appreciated property, regardless of the original cost basis;

- convert your low-yield property into a high income investment guaranteed to provide you and your spouse the financial security of lifetime income, immediate or deferred, with greatly reduced income tax consequences;

- serve as a vehicle to receive the "roll over" of your qualified pension plan or Individual Retirement Account (IRA), increasing both retirement income and tax savings;

- provide you with an immediate substantial charitable income tax deduction against your taxes for the year in which the CRT is created;

- diminish estate and inheritance taxes on the donated property — and avoid the probate mess as well; and

- for your heirs, provide a greatly increased inheritance, financed by the tax savings and increased income your CRT will provide.

Sounds too good to be true — or to be legal in present day, tax-oppressed America? Believe us, it is true.

A point to keep in mind as you consider a CRT and its suitability for you, a charitable remainder trust is what is known in the law as an "irrevocable living trust," a concept we have already explained in detail in chapter 2.

Under the law, the income and assets of a revocable or irrevocable trust are subject at least to one-time state and federal death taxes at the grantor's death. The trust property is included in the grantor's gross estate for tax purposes.

This means the fair market value of all estate assets above $600,000 — the federal estate tax individual exemption amount — are taxed on a 1994 scale up to 55 percent, the exact tax percentage depending on the total size of the deceased's taxable estate, payable within nine months after death. But importantly, trusts can be arranged so that upon the subsequent deaths of named beneficiaries or their heirs, further death taxes are avoided, a savings for the eventual trust beneficiaries, although this helpful aspect is often remote in time.

The CRT Explained

The charitable remainder trust — the CRT, is a statutory device authorized by Congress allowing those people of wealth who wish to "do good" — to do very well indeed. As you will see, it is no wonder the CRT has such wide popularity among the tax paying cognoscenti.

The CRT is a tax-exempt irrevocable living trust with one or more living income beneficiaries, and one or more qualified tax-exempt charitable remaindermen, the existence of which is authorized by sections 664(c) and (d) of the Internal Revenue Code.

And remember "irrevocable" means what it says: the transferred property is no longer yours. As a general rule, most experts offer the opinion that for feasible operation, a CRT should start with assets worth at least $50,000; but others say as little as $20,000 is financially sound if the donor is young and the term of years for the trust is long, or if high-yield investments such as a mutual fund are pursued by the trust.

Although our discussion centers on living charitable remainder trusts, a CRT also can be created in a last will and testament. A "testamentary CRT" is relatively rare, with a testator directing that a named percentage of the value of the

4

trust be paid to the beneficiary for life, with the remainder afterward going to a qualified charitable organization. This arrangement allows the present value of the charity's deferred interest to be deducted from federal estate taxes.

The single most distinctive characteristic of the CRT, and the key to its associated tax and income benefits, is found in the identity of the ultimate beneficiary of the trust — the "remainderman", to use again that quaint English common law term. When a CRT has fulfilled its terms, run its legal course, and is ready to go out of business, the law says the remaining assets ("the charitable remainder") must go to a "qualified" tax-exempt charitable organization as defined by the Internal Revenue Code in sections 170(b)(1)(A) and 170(c), and IRS Regulations section 1.644-3(a)(6)(iv). (See also Rev. Rul. 80-38, 1980-1 C.B. 57).

Under the IRS Code the donor has the right to change the ultimate remaindermen at any time before final distribution of the trust. So long as one charity is replaced with another IRS "qualified" charitable organization, the CRT's tax exempt status remains secure. Here's a tip: if you have a specific charity in mind (and you probably do), get them to pay the creation costs of your CRT in return for your including in the trust declaration a waiver of your right to change remaindermen, making them the sure winners.

Calling the CRT a "qualified trust," is yet another name you will sometimes hear, meaning both that the CRT itself "qualifies" for its special tax status, and that the object of its ultimate charitable distribution is also a "qualified" tax exempt organization.

That Congress should be so generous in allowing the grantor of a CRT so many tax breaks is perfectly consistent with the historic background we discussed — using taxes and tax concessions not just for revenue purposes, but to promote policy objectives as well. In exchange for his or her ultimate gift to charity, the CRT donor avoids many of the onerous asset-depleting tax burdens otherwise imposed by government — all in the name of promoting "sweet charity" which, it is rightly said, "begins at home."

With the CRT, it certainly does.

Let us now explore some of these attractive tax advantages that flow from the creation of a CRT.

Goodbye Capital Gains Tax

It has become commonplace in America's quadrennial presidential election platforms for Republicans to call for reductions or repeal of the capital gains tax ("CGT") to stimulate investment and economic growth — while

Democrats demand the tax be increased as a means of redistributing unjust gains from those who have much, to those who do not.

Lost in all the political rhetoric is the long-established availability of the charitable remainder trust, an effective bypass of the capital gains tax for a settlor who donates his or her appreciated property to the trust. The law is well-established that a transfer of appreciated property to a CRT is not a sale or exchange on which a capital gains tax is imposed, according to IRS Revenue Ruling 55-275, 1955-1 CB 295.

Hopefully, investments in real estate or other forms of property eventually mature, appreciating in value but too often declining in earnings or yield. Before this process proceeds too far, the prudent investor looks for new areas of investment with greater yields. But one very real roadblock gives pause before selling low-yield property and reinvesting elsewhere; the federal capital gains tax, which at this writing is set at the confiscatory maximum level of 28 percent.

Various states of the Union get into the act with their own CGT, for example, California, where it is now set at 11 percent. This produces a combined federal-state CGT of a whopping 36 percent — plus it pushes the taxpayer into a higher income tax bracket and raises his income taxes courtesy of that old tax bite devil "bracket creep."

To illustrate more vividly, suppose you are lucky enough to own a building worth $1 million currently, with a fully-depreciated acquisition basis of $40,000 — a prescient value judgment you made years ago — but now with a horrific taxable capital gain of $960,000. This means a combined federal and state CGT liability (if you live in California) of $344,832! That leaves $655,168 to reinvest, and if the first year pays a 10 percent return (again, lucky you), you get $65,517 in income — fully taxable at current federal and state income tax levels.

And don't forget estate taxes. If you are in the 50 percent estate tax bracket, and are unfortunate enough to die soon after your sale, your heirs will only get $327,584 after paying an estate tax of $327,584. Not much left of that $1 million building. How discouraging for those who remain alive.

But if you create a charitable remainder trust, then donate the building to the tax-exempt CRT, you pay no capital gains tax at all — zero, nor does the CRT trustee who sells the building later. The entire proceeds from the sale go into the trust for reinvestment — $1 million, tax free as authorized by section 664(c) of the Internal Revenue Code. (The CRT assumes the donor's cost basis and the subsequent sale of the property by the trust results in a capital gain, but no tax is imposed — but see the related discussion of taxation of a beneficiary's CRT payout, below).

Remember that you will need a qualified appraisal of the value of real estate or any other property at the time of transfer to a CRT, and the trustee is required to report the transaction to the IRS. The transfer itself can be accomplished by a simple deed or quitclaim deed from the donor.

Of course low cost basis appreciated real property (either developed or undeveloped) is not the only candidate for donation to your CRT; it may be your closely-held family business that has skyrocketed in value over the years; it might be your personal residence that has done the same; or growth stocks or aggressive mutual funds that now would better be replaced with conservative, safe, high income investments.

A word about mortgaged property you might consider for donation to a CRT. Under IRS rules, if the property has been encumbered within five years prior to the proposed date of transfer to the trust, acceptance by the CRT, or any trust payment on the mortgage, would cause it to lose its tax-exempt status — and defeat the purpose of its creation. Or the transfer could receive tax treatment as a "bargain sale," making at least part of the appreciation immediately taxable to the donor as a capital gain. If the donor cannot pay off the mortgage before the transfer, there are possible ways to get around these obstacles, including a trust declaration provision forbidding the payment of mortgages, or the donor formally agreeing to assume all mortgage obligations personally.

There are some other qualifying factors you should consider concerning transfers of property to a CRT.

In the case of a successful closely held business of long duration, the original stock usually has a very low cost basis and selling it through the medium of the CRT will produce huge tax savings. The fact that the business is sold through a tax-free CRT allows you as seller (technically the CRT is the seller) to structure a more attractive purchase agreement for the buyer, perhaps conceding some business tax benefits that would essentially be wasted if retained by the CRT. These tax concessions can boost the business sales price and/or clinch the deal. In this light, be sure to compare our discussion of trusts qualifying to hold title subchapter "S" corporation shares in chapter 6.

A CRT donation works with personal property also. Suppose you own a significant collection of art. Naming the art museum as the remainderman of your CRT provides you with leverage on keeping the collection together and its display.

You can also sell your home through a CRT. The law says people over 55 years of age are entitled to a one-time $125,000 capital gains exclusion on the sale of their home, if they re-invest the proceeds in a new home. If your home exceeds this $125,000 exclusion in value, you can sell it through a CRT and shelter all the income from the sale. This maneuver is known as a "charitable buy-down" in sophisticated real estate circles.

The possibilities of legal tax avoidance and significant guaranteed income are as limitless as the assets available for transfer to a CRT.

But be careful of greed. The IRS has warned it will disqualify a charitable remainder trust if the major reason for its creation is to avoid capital gains taxes. The IRS gave an example of a two-year unitrust that would pay 80 percent of its value to the settlor in one year and is funded soley with highly appreciated property. When the trust sold the property in the second year, meaning in theory the donor would receive the income tax free, the IRS advanced several theories to disqualify what it said was a "flagrant donor-serving" trust.

An Immediate Charitable Tax Deduction

In addition to escaping the capital gains tax, as settlor/donor of property to a CRT, you will receive an immediate personal charitable tax deduction from your income tax for your donated property in the year in which the transfer is made.

The amount of the total tax deduction allowed is that of the present fair market value of the projected remainder interest. This calculation is based on several variables: IRS life expectancy tables and the age of the indicated life beneficiary (or the term of years for which the CRT is created); the current assumed IRS midterm discount interest rate; the fair market value of the property itself; the percentage or fixed payout rate you choose for your life income payments from the CRT.

For example, take that $1 million building as a CRT gift. Using a life expectancy of twenty years, a 1992 IRS midterm discount rate, and a 10 percent payout rate (easy for purpose of arithmetic, but unlikely in today's low interest rate environment), you would have a $135,203 income tax deduction to be applied against a maximum of 30 percent of your adjusted gross income for the year. If the deduction causes you to exceed the 30 percent ceiling on total deductions, you can carry over the excess for up to five succeeding years.

In an instance where the property donated to the CRT is only slightly increased in value (it must be held for at least one year in order to qualify as a long-term capital gain), the donor can elect to base his or her tax deduction on the actual cost basis, in which case they are allowed total deductions of up to 50 percent of their adjusted gross income. If the asset has been held for more than one year, its full appreciated value must be used as the basis for calculating the available tax deduction limited to 30 percent.

In some cases, as when two spouses are to be the life beneficiaries, establishing two CRTs and splitting the gift, making each spouse a sole beneficiary, can greatly increase the income tax deduction. If the CRT declaration terms permit, as they should, additional contributions can be made to the trust at any time, and the income tax deductions allowed for that year will be based on the current age of the beneficiary.

As a general rule, property transferred to a CRT will be completely free of any federal gift taxes or estate taxes for the settlor/donor, so long as the donor and his or her spouse are the sole life beneficiaries.

Tax Exempt Family Foundations

A trend that may increase the attraction of the charitable remainder trust is the U.S. Congress' constant fiddling with the tax code.

While CRTs are not in any danger, as of January 1, 1995 the tax avoidance value of contributions of appreciated property to a tax-exempt qualified family foundation underwent a profound change. Prior to that date the worth of such gifts was calculated at current market value for charitable income tax deduction purposes. Now they will be valued only at original cost to the donor, a considerable come down in tax advantage. The prospects of a congressional move to repeal this change are uncertain at best.

Of course such appreciated property gifts can obtain full current market value deductibility if donated to a qualified CRT, and in a sense, while the money saved may not go to a family foundation, it will still be "all in the family."

Taxation of CRT Income

This tax discussion raises an important point constantly to be kept in mind: cash distributions to life beneficiaries of a CRT are taxable under a special three-tier income tax provision: first, as ordinary income to the beneficiary, if the trust has ordinary income; second, as a capital gain to the extent the trust has such a gain not taxed previously to the beneficiaries; and, third, as tax-free income, or a return of principal, if the distribution is in excess of ordinary income or capital gain.

Imposition of these beneficiary payout taxes suggests there may be an advantage to selling an appreciated asset first, then donating the cash proceeds to the CRT, thus assuring all future trust income will be tax free to the donor. When a CRT sells appreciated property, every subsequent annual distribution to beneficiaries in excess of ordinary income will be taxed as a capital gain, until the entire amount of the beneficiaries' original capital gain is paid. This means you may not escape some of the capital gains tax, but any payments are delayed and on the installment plan, and contingent on the type and amount of income the trust has.

The obvious solution is to fund the CRT with cash or non-appreciated assets allowing the trustee to invest in municipal bonds or securities that provide little or no current income, so there will be no immediate capital gains tax.

As you shall see in discussion that follows, there are several ways of structuring trust investments and income to minimize the beneficiary's income tax on annual payouts.

CRTs — Two Types

The would-be donor contemplating the creation of a charitable remainder trust has two major types from which to choose, based on the technical form of payout desired in each case:

- A grantor retained annuity trust ("GRAT"), from which the donor receives a fixed annual dollar payout for a fixed number of years, or for a single lifetime or joint lifetimes (if married), for example, $80,000 a year, or a flat annual payment of eight percent of $1 million transferred to the trust. This annuity CRT more often is the choice of older persons wishing a dependable fixed income without being subjected to nerve-racking investment ups and downs.

- A standard grantor retained "unitrust" ("GRUT"), or simply a "unitrust" as the most commonly used CRT is called, under which the donor receives for a similar period of time a fixed percentage of the trust assets, the exact dollar value of which must be determined annually, usually on the first of each year. For example, if the trust value increases from $1 million to $2 million, eight percent payments will double from $80,000 to $160,000.

Any good financial planner will usually recommend the unitrust because of the inflationary impact on an annuity trust. Even with current relatively low annual rates of inflation (as compared to the wild Jimmy Carter years in the 1970s with 18 percent inflation), the value of an annuity trust still declines rapidly. At four percent annual inflation, a fixed annuity will lose about one third of its real value in a ten-year period.

The IRS Says

The Internal Revenue Code imposes strict requirements on a CRT, including:

- an irrevocable transfer of property to the trust, which must be reported by the settlor/donor and the trust on IRS forms;

- payment by the trust of a certain percentage of the value of the trust assets to one or more non-charitable beneficiaries for a period measured by their lifetimes, or up to a maximum of twenty years;

- minimal payments of at least 5 percent of the value of the trust assets to the beneficiaries, a percentage that once chosen, cannot be changed during the life of the trust, as stated in section 664(d)(2) of the Internal Revenue Code;

- the remaining trust principal must be distributed to one or more qualified tax-exempt charitable institutions when the trust terminates — this being the key provision of a CRT.

Better Than A Pension Plan

There is also a popular variation of the unitrust usually called an "income only unitrust," which, after initial trust creation, can defer payment until a later date, thereby supplementing or substituting for a pension plan. (See Treasury Regulations, sec. 1.644-3(a)(1)(i)(b)). This type of CRT has become a very popular method of constructing a favorable low-tax retirement income fund.

As we have seen, the law requires distribution to beneficiaries of an amount equal to at least 5 percent of the trust assets each year, and in a typical unitrust the beneficiary must receive the annual payment, even if principal has to be invaded to make that payment. But this requirement can be waived if the trust declaration includes a direction that payments are to be made from trust "income only."

With careful planning and administration, the cash proceeds from the sale of original appreciated trust property can be reinvested in valuable assets producing little or no income in the early years of the trust operation, even as they increase in total value because of tax-free compounding.

Years later, when the beneficiary desires income for retirement, these low-yield trust assets can be sold, and funds shifted to high-yield investments paying the beneficiary the lesser of the fixed percentage of the value of trust assets, or from trust income which exceeds this percentage, for as long as he or she lives.

There can and should also be a "make up" provision in the trust declaration, requiring that whenever the specified percentage is not paid in any year because of the "income only" limitation forbidding invasion of principal, the cumulative deficit owed will be made up by increased payments in the subsequent years in which trust income does exceed the specified percentage of value.

Unlike 401K, Keogh, IRAs or other retirement plans, there is no limit to the amount one can contribute to a "net income" CRT, and some donor/beneficiaries continue to contribute on a monthly or other periodic basis until they need payback.

The Payout Rate — What and How

- Once you have chosen the unitrust route of tax breaks and increased income, two decisions have to be made — bearing in mind that under IRS rules these decisions, once made, are *irrevocable* for the life of the CRT:

- Recognizing that the IRS requires a minimum payout rate of 5 percent in order for a CRT to qualify, what payout rate do you want or need?

- How will you deal with the net income limitation?

Factors to Consider

Here are some of the variables you should take into account before choosing the payout rate and the net income limitation; your age and that of your spouse, if you are married; the age of any other beneficiaries of the trust, assuming these may include your present or later born children; the fair market value of the appreciated asset you transfer to the CRT, and your tax basis in that asset; calculation of a reasonable rate of return on the re-invested proceeds after the assets are sold; the likely rate of inflation and the degree of anti-inflation protection you want built in by allowing tax-free compounding of value; the total amount of other assets and income you will have available, other than the CRT payback.

Lastly, you should also determine the cost of future insurance premiums (or a one time premium), if you decide to create a life insurance trust for your heirs — about which we will have more to say in chapter 7.

A good CRT attorney and/or investment advisor should be able to draw a complete picture of the personal situation of each client based on information about the above factors, then provide an accurate dollar projection of how much your immediate charitable tax deduction will be, to what extent your annual income will increase each year, how much you will be able to leave your heirs, and what will be the eventual bequest you make to your chosen charities.

Choosing the Payout Rate

Let's consider first the decision concerning establishing the payout rate itself.

If your immediate need is for high income levels, choosing a relatively high payout rate makes some sense. But if you are a settlor/donor beginning retirement, you should choose a payout rate that leaves sufficient funds in the CRT each year to keep your trust income ahead of projected inflation.

One approach would be to specify a relatively high payout rate, say 8 percent, and permit payment to be made from principal if trust net income is insufficient to meet this obligation to the beneficiary. In such a case investment would be almost entirely for growth purposes and well-capitalized growth stocks might be the place to look.

Over the past 50 years, the best U.S. stocks have produced a return averaging about 12.7 percent annually. With an 8 percent payout and a growth stock investment policy, after administrative costs, it can reasonably be expected that about 4 percent of the fund could be added to trust principal each year.

The difficulty with this approach is that the annual rate of return left in the CRT each year must at least equal or surpass the annual rate of inflation, in order to preserve the purchasing power of future distributions and the ultimate remainder interest. An equal problem will be that annual payouts will be highly variable from year to year, because of inevitable fluctuations in the stock market. The donor/beneficiary must be willing to put up with this variable payout prospect as the price of higher investment income.

Economic realities in the U.S. and the world will make it difficult, if not impossible, to produce a gross income return in excess of 8 percent, even if the CRT portfolio is invested totally in fixed income holdings, assuming the purchase of investment grade debt instruments. Expenses chargeable to income must also be subtracted, so the net income is likely to be even lower. For comparison's sake, consider that the highest quality long term bond yields have historically averaged about 4 to 5 percent a year. Assuming that your CRT will hold long term bonds to maturity, this part of the trust principal will not grow with inflation. Remember that if your CRT principal does not grow, neither does the income of the beneficiaries.

As an illustration of what happens when these factors are applied to CRT investment, a good case can be made that a conservative 5 percent payout rate will have the best all around results in the long term, **if** there is the right mix of investments and careful management.

Assume in year one $1 million available for investment; a total trust investment mix of about 40 percent bonds with an annual 7 percent rate of return, 30 percent Standard and Poors 500 stocks with a return of 12.7 percent, and another 30 percent split evenly between fast-growing U.S. and international small equities with rates of return of about 15 to 16 percent plus. Under this investment mix, with a 5 percent CRT payout rate, the $1 million will blossom in 20 years to about $4,800,000, of which $2,326,000 will be paid out to the beneficiaries.

Compare this with the choice of a higher 7 percent CRT payout rate; the same $1 million invested totally in safe no-growth long term bonds at 7 percent net annual return, in 20 years will leave only $1 million in principal, after cumulative annual beneficiary payments of $1.4 million.

Check that comparative 20-year record again: a 5 percent payout rate with a carefully mixed investment policy produces $2.3 million in benefits; a 7 percent payout rate with a no growth investment policy produces $1.4 million in benefits. The 5 percent choice ends up with $4.8 million remainder for charity, the 7 percent, only $1 million — each with concomitant charitable income tax deductions for the donor in the first year based on the rate of payout chosen in year one. In effect, you control the amount of your tax deduction by your choice of the CRT payout rate.

The Net Income Limitation

The second major initial decision for the donor is how to deal with the net income limitation on the CRT payout.

The decision here will largely depend on your CRT investment policy, how immediate your need for income may be, or whether you wish to postpone income until a later time. There are four possibilities:

(1) Require annual payout whether or not there is net income sufficient to pay it, i.e. take some out of principal. But keep in mind what happens then. The effect of failing to meet a required payout by even a small percentage over many years has some dramatic results. Assuming $1 million invested, an 8 percent payout and a 7 percent overall investment return, the principal would shrink to $739,700 in 30 years.

(2) Limit annual payout to available net income, but include a "catch up" provision allowing shortfalls to be paid later out of future year excess income. This is convenient for younger donors who don't want much income early in the life of the trust, later switching to high income growth stocks when they retire. This "growth without income" strategy early-on can be accomplished by investing in growth securities, zero coupon bonds and deferred annuities. In effect, this is using an appreciated asset to fund a pension plan substitute, without

all the reporting and restrictions imposed on pension plans.

(3) Limit annual payout to the lowest of either the established annual payout amount or, the available net income. If the CRT is funded with non-liquid assets like closely held corporation stock or real estate with little current income, this option is the best.

(4) Impose no net income limitations, thereby leaving open the possibility of employing a more growth oriented investment approach to produce an increased total return. This makes sense when the CRT is funded with liquid assets which can easily be invested and re-invested — and when there is full-time, careful management.

These sorts of multi-year dollar projections are easily done by computer and should be available before choosing the rate of return and any net income limitations. Also note that when we use the phrase "annual payout" in all of these alternatives, that includes the possibility you may elect to have payments semi-annually or quarterly, both of which are common.

The "bottom line" as they say, on these choices is that while a CRT is a very useful investment device, in order to be successful the donor has to take a hard-eyed look at future economic realities, including inflation and long-term rates of return, before choosing an approach that matches the donor's goals. It also means consideration of a lower payout rate, which may easily be more productive in the long haul.

On a related point, trust donors can establish a longer term CRT that benefits them during their lives, then afterwards benefits successor generations of children and grandchildren. This has the effect of maximizing the cumulative impact of tax-free compounding of value. Careful planning must go into such an arrangement in order to avoid adverse estate tax and generation-skipping transfer taxes, but it can be done — and the many years of compounding makes it all worthwhile.

Investing Trust Assets In A Commercial Annuity

The trustee could immediate sell the appreciated assets transferred to the trust and invest the proceeds in a commercial annuity. The investment strategy would be to grow the annuity fund as much as possible during the pre-retirement years. To accomplish this, the trustee would choose a deferred annuity.

Because the trust is not a "natural person," annual increases in the value of the annuity would be treated as constructive receipt of income by the trust. The trust agreement would have to define income for trust accounting and distribution purposes so as to include only income actually received by the trust. As a result, there would be no trust income and no need to make distributions during the pre-retirement years.

However, if an income were needed or panted prior to retirement, the trustee could simply withdraw amounts from the annuity and, assuming the fund had grown in value, the full amount of the withdrawal would be trust income and could be immediately distributed — up to the income value limit of the trust in that year plus any accumulated deficits.

After retirement, the trustee could withdraw a reasonable amount each year to provide a lifetime retirement income.

Role of the Trustee

Earlier we talked about the importance of the trustee in any trust, but as you can readily understand from this discussion of charitable remainder trust investment policy, the role of the CRT trustee is crucial to success. While trust management can be complex and time consuming, in most situations an individual trustee can usually handle the work with occasional assistance from an attorney or investment planner.

There is a natural tendency on the part of a settlor/donor to want to serve as his or her own CRT trustee, and the law does not forbid this dual role. However, as noted before, this arrangement immediately raises questions of conflict of interest, especially about the character of investments the trustee may choose. A donor who does not serve as trustee still has a significant degree of continuing control, because the donor can reserve the right in the trust declaration to change the trustee at any time. The donor can also ask the trustee to change the nature of the CRT investments from low-yield growth assets to high income investments, at any time the donor/beneficiary needs steady income.

Realistically, the creation and operation of a CRT usually means there is a close working relationship between the donor/ beneficiary and their personally chosen trustee. In a serious dispute, the beneficiary can always look to the courts to protect his or her interests, if the trustee is thought to be engaged in activity inimicable to the best interests of the trust.

The duties of a CRT trustee include selling at the best price possible the appreciated assets transferred to the trust; investing the proceeds from the sale in the manner that will best advance the trust goals; arranging the cash flow needed for periodic distributions to beneficiaries; annual evaluation of trust assets; filing federal trust tax forms (IRS forms 1041A and 5227); maintaining a trust bank account and accurate records of income, expenses, payouts and accumulations of income and capital gains; and, informing beneficiaries of how they must personally report annual payouts for tax purposes.

For obvious reasons, if the donor/beneficiary does serve as a trustee, it is highly advisable to have a co-trustee with full authority to make the annual value determination required in a unitrust CRT, so there will be no question about impartiality.

As an established rule of thumb, annual costs of trust administration should be less than 2 percent of the value of the trust, or something is wrong somewhere.

The CRT and the "Prudent Investor" Rule

Earlier we discussed the rules governing trust investment policy in general. Keep in mind that the trustee must act in a fiduciary capacity on behalf of the interests of both parties to the CRT — the donor/beneficiary and the remainderman. This means an impartial administration of trust assets to provide both favorable current income, and also preservation of the largest possible remaining corpus for the designated charity.

You might want to refresh your memory concerning the "prudent investor" rule discussed in chapter 3.

For example, a trust arrangement which allows the beneficiary to receive payment out of principal when current income is insufficient, clearly harms the interest of the remainderman — an inherent conflict of interest for the trustee. This dilemma can be avoided so long as the overall rate of return (current income plus capital appreciation) meets the payout requirement, and thus keeps the corpus intact. But when the trustee must figure in inflation, principal may have to be invaded to pay the beneficiary. As we have already discussed, setting the payout rate at the minimum 5 percent will usually avoid this conflict, but higher payout rates might guarantee the problem.

The practical solution is to set the payout rate as low as possible (5 percent, the minimum the IRS permits), so that an experienced trustee's wisely diversified portfolio of investments can earn interest and dividends sufficient to meet all current income needs with inflation taken into account.

Don't forget in this discussion of "competing interests" between CRT beneficiaries and the remainderman; the sole policy reason the law allows and encourages charitable remainder trusts (and the concomitant benefits to donors), is the ultimate objective of promoting charitable organizations and the achievement of their goals by tax-exempt private financing. The IRS does not look favorably on operating a sham CRT providing bountiful lifetime rewards to its donor/beneficiary, while ultimately short changing the charitable organization it was created to help. Follow that route and it leads to enormous retroactive tax liabilities, including interest and penalties stretching back over the years to the CRT's date of creation.

In the midst of all these shifting variables, the "prudent investor" trustee can easily get caught "in the middle." These problems should suggest how important it is to choose a qualified CRT trustee who, in fact, has your complete trust.

Taking Care of the Children

There are solid practical reasons why a CRT should have as its life beneficiaries a husband and wife, and not their children. These reasons are taxes.

If the sole individual CRT beneficiary is the settlor/donor, federal law exempts the entire value of the property donated to the CRT from all federal gift and estate taxes. This tax avoidance is a considerable advantage, at a time when both these federal taxes are assessed at up to 55 percent of the total value of the estate property. If the donor's spouse is also a beneficiary, the value of that interest is reportable as a taxable gift, but it fully qualifies for a marital gift tax deduction of $600,000.

If the couples' children (or others) are also named as beneficiaries, their interests are taxable gifts to the extent their interests exceed the allowable annual exclusions. Annual gifts of cash or other property worth $10,000 or less, often called "annual exclusion gifts," may be made by a donor free of any federal gift or estate tax. In order to qualify for this exclusion the gift must be of a "present interest" in the property. Trust gifts do not usually qualify unless the trust is specially designed to accommodate such "present interest" gifts — make sure your trust expert addresses that need.

In addition to federal estate and gift taxes, any grandchildren's CRT interest would also be subject to the federal "generation skipping" tax of a flat 55 percent in excess of $1 million in gifts made to them during the donor's lifetime. One bright spot is that property given to a qualified charity is fully deductible against any gift or estate taxes.

If one does not include their children as beneficiaries of the CRT, how does one "make it up" to the kids for their "lost" value of the $1 million building that ultimately becomes a gift to the charitable remainderman?

There are several ways to accomplish this worthy parental goal, but first let's consider some simple tax arithmetic to lay a basis for a suggested solution.

When a building (or anything else) valued at $1 million is donated to a CRT, it is received tax free. As we have seen, with a capital gains tax the $1 million would have been reduced to $731,200 in after tax cash. But $1 million invested by the CRT at an expected 8 percent return gives the donor $80,000 annually in income, rather than $58,496, the annual amount of cash after the capital gains tax. That means a net bonanza of $21,504 each year. And here's where the solution to the children's inheritance problem is achieved.

Using $15,000 of the net bonanza money, the parents can fund an irrevocable life insurance trust, (also called a "wealth replacement" or inheritance trust), with their children as named beneficiaries. We will have more to say about such a trust in chapter 7.

Many couples chose to have their life insurance trust purchase a "last to die" or "survivorship" policy covering them jointly. Such a policy is much cheaper and is not payable, as indicated, until the last of the two parents dies. Donating a portion of their increased income from their CRT to their life insurance trust, about $15,000 annually, for ten years will allow purchase of a "last to die" whole life policy paying about $750,000. This inheritance is far more than the net value that $1 million building would have produced had it not gone to the CRT, but remained a part of the parents' estate to be ravaged by federal taxes.

The $750,000 insurance payout figure is approximate because, as in all insurance policies, the exact premiums and payout depends on variables concerning the person or persons insured. This figure is a quote from an insurance company based on a non-smoking 65 year-old couple in good health at the time the life insurance is purchased. Some insurance companies will include an optional clause guaranteeing that if both insured parents die within four years of each other, the company will pay out 222 percent of the face value of the policy. At least one spouse must be under age 70 and in good health to obtain this lucrative policy rider, but that means double the money for your heirs.

Even if the IRS somehow successfully attacked this sum as being taxable as part of the parents' estate, and even if the estate was in the 55 percent tax bracket, that means on a $1 million policy paying $2.22 million, after tax proceeds would still equal the $1 million. It's worth the gamble and probably more likely than winning the state lottery.

Using the life insurance trust route, every body should be pleased; the parents have added net lifetime income from the CRT, the children have an equal or greater inheritance, and the charity of your choice benefits greatly in the end.

A word of caution. Before establishing a life insurance trust and having it purchase any life insurance policies, all the personal health variables, actual premium costs and payouts should be realistically assessed and quotations obtained in writing from the prospective insurer. This is not an area to be left to hopeful promises from an eager insurance salesperson.

After all, your children deserve the best — guaranteed money.

Make the Most of Your IRA with a CRT

A charitable remainder trust can also be used in conjunction with an IRA or other retirement plan to minimize estate taxes and completely avoid income taxes on the IRA, while also providing excellent lifetime income to family members and - the ultimate benefit to your favorite qualified charity.

Retirement plans and their cash value present a major headache to estate planners because, unlike most assets, the beneficiaries who receive these assets must pay income taxes as would the decedent. This means that between estate and income taxes, the cash value remaining in an IRA or other plan can be depleted by as much as 75 percent - and even more if the decedent is subject to the 15 percent excess accumulation tax.

For example, consider an estate in which the major asset is an IRA account valued at $720,000. At the account owner's death the full value of the IRA would be included in the gross estate for federal estate tax purposes. The federal tax on a total estate of $1.6 million, including the IRA, would be $408,000. Without the IRA, it would be only $106,000. Of course there would also be state death taxes to consider.

You can easily understand why another, low-tax way to treat the IRA must be found.

The solution is to establish a testamentary charitable remainder trust in your will, naming the trust as the death beneficiary of your IRA or other retirement plan. The IRA agreement should also be amended to name the CRT as the sole successor beneficiary of the IRA. This not only avoids huge estate and income taxes, it removes the major hassle of complying with IRA rules and regulations.

Fortunately, in 1994 the IRS issued a series of private letter rulings stating; 1) a CRT can be the beneficiary of an IRA; 2) because the CRT is tax-exempt, the trust can withdraw the proceeds of an IRA completely tax-free, and; 3) the present value of an IRA received by a CRT qualifies for the estate tax charitable deduction.

In such an arrangement, an IRA account holder can name children and grandchildren (or any persons living when the CRT comes into existence) as beneficiaries. The will provisions establishing the IRA-CRT can also chose the annuity trust, or the more common unitrust form for the CRT. Under the unitrust choice, that trust would withdraw the IRA funds as soon as possible after death and re-invest them in growth securities or other holdings designed to produce an average annual yield of 12 percent or more, guaranteeing income for the beneficiaries.

One of the adult beneficiaries can be named as co-trustee with primary investment authority, and to simplify things, the other co-trustee can be the qualified charity that eventually receives the remainder interest. Most such named charities will assume the paperwork, tax returns, accounting and other administration at no cost under such an arrangement.

If an IRA is the major asset in your estate, this is the way to minimize income and estate taxes and maximize a guaranteed high lifetime income to your chosen heirs.

Internationalizing Your CRT

The CRT can be a foreign trust, but it is not permitted to be a "grantor trust." Any non-U.S. trust created by a U.S. person which has a U.S. beneficiary is automatically a "grantor trust." But, for CRT purposes only, the status of the donor/grantor and his spouse are ignored.

The CRT can be a foreign trust yet not be a grantor trust if the only U.S. beneficiary of the trust is either the grantor or his spouse. But a non-U.S. corporation can be the beneficiary, and this is the solution recommended by most international tax planners. An international, albeit foreign charity, might be named as the recipient of the remainder interest. The prospective charity would be located in a U.S. possession, which is not deemed to be a part of the United States (see Code Section 7701(a)(9), but does qualify under Section 170(c) to receive the remainder interest. The charity does not need to be named. The CRT need only provide that the charity must be a non-U.S. entity which nonetheless qualifies under Code Section 170(c).

This brief summary of internationalizing a CRT only begins to touch on the complexities of the subject, but in combination with other entities, including the hybrid company, the international CRT can be an excellent way of removing appreciated asset values from the U.S.

In Summary

Because the tax code is constantly being changed by Congress, there is never any assurance the multiple benefits of charitable remainder trusts will always be available in its present form. With so many donors, beneficiaries and charitable organizations all giving and receiving many hundreds of millions of dollars every year under this system, it is unlikely such a popular and long standing feature of tax law will be changed substantially. But like the recent limitation imposed on gifts of appreciated property to family foundations, the CRT also can be modified to curb its benefits.

One last suggestion: while we do not recommend you set up your own CRT without expert assistance, you should know the IRS provides approved CRT creation forms developed by the IRS for that purpose. Properly filled out, these forms assure IRS approval of the CRT.

The moral of this story — the time is now for you to investigate and decide whether the charitable remainder trust is the right way to go for you, your family and your favorite charity. If it is — act now.

The Charitable Lead Trust

A few words about a related charitable trust, but one that works in the reverse way from a CRT known, as a "charitable lead trust."

Here the settlor donates valuable assets to a trust to be held for a set number of years, during which income from the assets is paid by the trust to qualified charitable groups you may choose. When the chosen term of years ends, the asset is transferred to the settlor/donor's beneficiaries, but with greatly reduced estate and gift taxes reflecting the prior distributions to charity.

This trust is really only useful if the principal assets are of very great value, which they must be in order to produce continuing substantial trust income for the charitable beneficiary. Also setup and operating costs are considerable, all factors making this a trust for the very wealthy who want to keep an asset in the family while greatly reducing the tax costs of passing it on. The late Jackie Kennedy Onassis used the charitable lead trust technique to shelter about 90 percent of her trust assets from estate and gift taxes.

About the Author

Over the past 25 years, Adam Starchild has been the author of over two dozen books, and hundreds of magazine articles, primarily on business and finance. His articles have appeared in a wide range of publications around the world -- including Business Credit, Euromoney, Finance, The Financial Planner, International Living, Offshore Financial Review, Reason, Tax Planning International, The Bull & Bear, Trust & Estates, and many more.

Now semi-retired, he was the president of an international consulting group specializing in banking, finance and the development of new businesses, including tourist enterprises. He has owned and operated travel agencies, travel wholesalers, and tour operators.

Although this formidable testimony to expertise in his field, plus his current preoccupation with other books-in-progress, would not seem to leave time for a well-rounded existence, Starchild has won two Presidential Sports Awards and written several cookbooks, and is currently involved in a number of personal charitable projects.

His personal website is at http://www.adamstarchild.com/